Simon Nasht's

Frank Hurley – The Man Who Made History

Study notes for Area of Study:
Discovery 2015–2018 HSC

Bruce Pattinson

A
FIVE SENSES
PUBLICATION

Five Senses Education Pty Ltd
2/195 Prospect Highway
Seven Hills 2147
New South Wales
Australia

First Published 2015

Pattinson, Bruce
Top Notes – Frank Hurley – The Man Who Made History
ISBN 978-1-74130-186-1

CONTENTS

TOP NOTES SERIES

This series has been created to assist HSC students of English in their understanding of set texts. Top Notes are easy to read, provide analysis of issues and discuss important ideas contained in the texts.

Particular care has been taken to ensure students are able to examine each text in the context of the Area of Study or module and elective to which it has been allocated.

Each text generally includes:

- Notes on the specific module
- Plot summary
- Character analysis
- Setting
- Thematic concerns
- Language studies
- Essay questions and a modelled response
- Other textual material
- Practice questions
- Useful quotes

We have covered the areas we feel are important for students in their study of Discovery for their Area of Study. I am sure you will find these Top Notes useful in your studies of English.

Bruce Pattinson
Series Editor

AREA OF STUDY: DISCOVERY

'We learn wisdom from failure much more than from success. We often discover what will do, by finding out what will not do; and probably he who never made a mistake never made a discovery.'

SAMUEL SMILES

The Area of Study set for the 2015–18 HSC is *Discovery*. It is compulsory to study this topic as prescribed by the Board of Studies. Remember you are supposed to analyse your texts with reference to varying aspects of *Discovery*. Markers will be looking to see evidence of deep conceptual understanding of the Area of Study and you are encouraged to support your views with close textual referencing.

In the Area of Study you will be analysing many texts that are related to the idea of discovery. You will analyse texts not only to investigate the ideas they present about this area but also how they deliver these ideas. This means you will be looking closely at the techniques composers use to represent ideas and shape meaning. You will also be looking at relationships between texts. Overall, you will become an expert on discovery- the different notions people have about it and the various ways composers manipulate techniques to communicate their ideas about the topic. The material in this Top Note will help you do that.

Specifically you will look at:

- A set text from the following list of fourteen texts. **You will only study one of these.**
  - *Wrack* – James Bradley
  - *The Awakening* – Kate Chopin
  - *A Short History of Nearly Everything* – Bill Bryson
  - *The Motorcycle Diaries* – Ernesto 'Che' Guevara
  - *Swallow the Air* – Tara June Winch
  - *Away* – Michael Gow
  - *Rainbow's End* – Jane Harrison
  - *Frank Hurley - The Man Who Made History* – Simon Nasht
  - *Life of Pi* – Ang Lee
  - *The Tempest* – William Shakespeare
  - *Selected Poems* – Robert Gray
  - *Selected Poems* – Rosemary Dobson
  - *Selected Poems* – Robert Frost
  - *Go Back To Where You Came From* – selected episodes – Ivan O'Mahoney
- Additional related texts of your own choosing.

You must write about your set text and additional texts of your own choosing in the first English paper of the HSC examination.

I hope that posterity will judge me kindly, not only as to the things which I have explained, but also to those which I have intentionally omitted so as to leave to others the pleasure of discovery.

RENE DESCARTES

WHAT DOES THE BOARD OF STUDIES REQUIRE FOR THE AREA OF STUDY?

The Board of Studies documentation says of the Area of Study: Discovery that it;

> *'requires students to explore the ways in which the concept of discovery is represented in and through texts.' (p 9)*

The document English Stage 6 Prescriptions: Area of Study Electives and Texts (August 2013) notes that perceptions of discovery can encompass many things and are shaped by context.

- Students can consider –not only discovery but also rediscovery.
- That discovery may be planned or unplanned and may lead to new worlds and values.
- Discoveries can question and challenge and lead to different conclusions.

You will also need to consider that the 'process of discovering can vary according to personal, cultural, historical and social contexts and values.'

Below is an abbreviated version of what the Board requires of students.

'In their responses and compositions students examine, question, reflect and speculate on':

- their own experiences of discovery, personally and through texts.

- the assumptions underlying the representations of discovery.
- the effects of composers' choices of techniques.
- the ways in which the study of discovery has helped them understand the world and themselves.

Think carefully about the wording that is used so that you can adopt this language for your own work.

If this is what is required by the Board of Studies you need to examine the concept of discovery carefully so you can respond adequately. We would recommend that you read the complete document which is on the Board of Studies website (http://www.bostes.nsw.edu.au) and can be downloaded in Word or PDF formats.

UNDERSTANDING THE AREA OF STUDY

'There is no better high than discovery'

- E. O. WILSON

Discovery is often associated with adventure. The word *Discovery* conjures childhood dreams of exotic locations, intrepid explorers in jungles discovering lost tribes and great treasures. Movies embrace this theme. The Discovery Channel exists to help people to discover facts vicariously. The concept behind the never-ending Star Trek series is to 'explore strange new worlds, to seek out new life and new civilisations, to boldly go where no man has gone before'.

Even the self-discovery/self-help industry is a major one in all the nations of earth; people are willing to make great sacrifices to discover the 'truth' about themselves and the world. All this is undoubtedly true but discovery is much more than this and we will need to have a broader and more sophisticated understanding to undertake our studies of the texts set for study.

The Board of Studies has outlined in their documentation: students are required to 'explore the ways in which the concept of discovery is represented in and through texts'. (p 9 *HSC Prescriptions 2015–20 English Stage 6*). This is our first step and it indicates that we must pay particular attention to the text and its content and techniques, particularly the techniques the composer uses to engage the audience and convey the main purpose of their text.

The whole aim of this Area of Study is to examine the text closely but also relate it to the idea of discovery and decide how examining it in this way enables us to better understand both the text and the concept. It is important that you formulate your own ideas about the text and attempt to develop some original and creative ideas about what you are studying.

The Board's documentation should be read in full and the annotations document should also be examined for the particular texts you are studying as this document offers insights into the way each particular text should be examined by outlining key ideas and areas for clarification.

The *Prescriptions* document states on the Area of Study that *Discovery* can be:

- something new
- a rediscovery
- sudden, unexpected
- carefully planned
- 'fresh and intensely meaningful in ways that may be emotional, creative, intellectual, physical and spiritual.' (p9)

- confronting
- provocative
- enable speculation

It can:

- change perceptions of individuals and groups.
- create new values

The document also suggests that discoveries and ways of discovering vary due to individual circumstance and that these discoveries can change many things about lives, communities and the world(s). Of course when we examine the concept of discovery we need to examine how 'discovering' the text itself may change us and how we view things. The text may challenge and confront and change how we see the human experience.

Students can also think about 'their own experiences of discovery' and how a composer's choice of form, feature and language influences their views of discovery. Examining and enjoying any text is a discovery in itself but it is what we take away from the text and apply that is the real discovery. That is not to say that every text will be enjoyed or offer a discovery. Some may not personally engage you and that is fine. This is especially so when you begin to find other related material that links to Discovery. Find examples of texts that link in significant ways to your prescribed text.

Defining Discovery

'Definition is the death of discovery'

-TOM SHADYAK

Now let's define discovery in a more coherent and easily understood way so we can begin our investigation at a basic level before moving into more complex analysis. Dictionary.com defines the term as:

1. The act or instance of discovering
2. Something discovered
3. In legal terms it is compulsory disclosure of evidence
4. The name of the third space shuttle.

Obviously the first three terms are more suitable but the final definition shows how pervasive the idea of discovery is and how it has influenced people over time. The search for the 'new' has driven much development over past millennia. Discoveries are always met with excitement and often trepidation as to what change they might bring.

Think historically about how people have reacted to change. It can cause great upheavals in society, with violent reactions while other changes brought through discoveries are welcomed and may save and enhance lives. Consider medical advancements, scientific developments and the ever-quickening world of the computer. Even the way I am creating this text in Evernote on an iPad would not have been possible twelve months ago. Discovery brings change and may affect different people or groups of people, even nations in various ways both positive and negative. It is pertinent now to examine some more definitions.

The word discover and its definition also sheds some light on the concept:

1. To see, get knowledge, to learn, to find, get knowledge of something previously seen or unknown.

As does the definition of the word discovering:

1. Noticing or realising.

These definitions all point to the fact that realisation is the key to discovery. This realisation may come unexpectedly, occasionally or never. Someone else may have the same experience and make the discovery. The realisation may be accidental or organised, take years in the planning or come as a complete surprise.

Discoveries can come in many ways and the synonyms for discover listed below help us to understand the concept even further. They assist in defining how a discovery can arise:

Synonyms – ascertain, catch, come upon, contrive, determine, design, dig up, disclose, elicit, explore, bring to light, unearth, encounter, experiment, invent, originate, expose, locate, perceive, sense, strike, verify.

These synonyms show partly the vast array of words that our language has created around this concept and show how important it is in the human psyche. Look also at the antonyms that show how we view not discovering things; lose, miss, pass by.

We, as a race, want to discover. Now we will look at some examples of discovery and examine their impact. It is also important to remember that discoveries do not have to be positive. You might discover you have a huge problem, an incurable illness, a strange past, an unwelcome relative or something equally bizarre. There may be a darker side to any discovery that could be addressed. Think about the effect of the white discoverers on indigenous populations.

Types of Discovery

Personal Discovery

'I think a spiritual journey is not so much a journey of discovery. It's a journey of recovery. It's a journey of uncovering your own inner nature. It's already there.'

BILLY CORGAN

The idea of personal discovery or self-discovery as many of the books also describe it, is a popular and pervasive concept. It is more prevalent in the developed nations of the world where people seek something more spiritual or meaningful rather than their consumer driven lives and the day to day grind of work. Many seek something more; they strive to discover something within or without, a better self, a way to live in the now or just a way to escape from reality. A huge amount of material (literature, DVDs, audiobooks) has been assembled to help individuals achieve their life goals.

Individuals seek to achieve personal discovery in a variety of ways. Some examples are courses and conferences where they are led through exercises, both physical and psychological, to develop new skills and discover their inner spirituality. Others join communities, religious groups or renounce material possessions and become itinerant travellers or, in old fashioned terms, 'hippies'. Through this they discover whatever they lack in their current state (hopefully) and become a better or more effective person. Others use these discoveries to enrich themselves or manage better in their existing lives. Whatever the reason or outcome, personal discovery is a huge industry and an integral part of our society.

For more information on this area you could investigate the self-help, self- improvement section of a book store or get on YouTube and type these terms in. You will get plenty of ideas and advice!

Inner Discovery

'The greatest discovery of my generation is that man can alter his life simply by altering his attitude of mind.'

JAMES ADAMS

The concept of inner discovery is closely aligned with the previous topic and can be seen similarly yet it is more aligned with exceptional circumstances. For example some people learn much about themselves during physical, emotional or psychologically stressful times and are astounded by the inner strength they have while others around them break down or fail to cope. Others find inner strength through meditation, retreats, or extremes such as becoming a hermit and focusing on the inner person. This concept of personal enlightenment is also a business in the modern world and you can get coaches who will work with you to find your inner self through various processes of discovery.

If you are looking for examples to use in your related material try googling the term and you will find a whole range of programs, coaches and books that will help you find your inner self. Dag Hammarskjold (former UN Secretary General) said 'The longest journey is the journey inwards. Of him who has chosen his destiny, who has started upon his quest for the source of his being.'

Discovery through Travel

The idea of discovery through travel is one of the first things that occur to people when they hear the word discovery. As Martin Buber (Austrian-born 20th Century Jewish philosopher) stated, 'All journeys have secret destinations of which the traveller is unaware'. This sense of travel enabling discoveries is well documented and became even more prominent as people began to sail widely across the seas to discover 'new' lands, many of which had been occupied by indigenous peoples for centuries. Travel was, and to some extent still is, associated with an adventure, a journey, to test the boundaries of what we already know and to see how far we can take the new experience and how it changes us. What we discover on our travels is revealing and often confronting.

> *Adventure is a path. Real adventure—self-determined, self-motivated, often risky—forces you to have firsthand encounters with the world. The world the way it is, not the way you imagine it. Your body will collide with the earth and you will bear witness. In this way you will be compelled to grapple with the limitless kindness and bottomless cruelty of humankind—and perhaps realise that you yourself are capable of both. This will change you. Nothing will ever again be black-and-white.*
>
> – **MARK JENKINS**
>
> (HTTP://MATADORNETWORK.COM/BNT/50-MOST-INSPIRING-TRAVEL-QUOTES-OF-ALL-TIME/#RCM3GIDFT04P07MB.99)

Discovery through travel brings this kind of change and it may involve understanding another culture, disrupting a prejudice or habit, making a friend or discovering some amazing natural beauty. Discovery through travel is one of the most written about and frequently mentioned ideas when discussing the concept. Travel has certainly changed over the centuries, even in the past decade travel to distant places has become commonplace. Air travel has especially become less than the special thing for the privileged or extremely adventurous that it was in the beginning. Think back to the times when to travel from place to place by foot or by horse was a major event. From the Middle Ages through to the later eighteenth century many people had never ventured beyond their village, apart from an infrequent trip to the nearest town. This idea leads us to consider the idea of the journey.

Discovery through Journey

This is an idea common to many areas of the discovery concept. Often the two words are associated if we think of the journey as a process not just a physical movement. Often discoveries are made on the journey rather than at the destination. The word journey has also been applied to abstract concepts. Lyndon Johnson, the American President, described peace as a deliberate process: 'Peace is a journey of a thousand miles and it must be taken one step at a time'. Many have heard the quote by Lao Tzu 'A journey of a thousand miles must begin with one step'.

The concept of journey leading to discovery is a constant in modern film and literature and it has been extensively studied in works such as Joseph Campbell's *The Hero's Journey*. This model organises the journey by stages which are common to all culture. Despite the cross-cultural commonalities, journeys allow discovery about self and such discoveries are individual.

As Marcel Proust (19th and 20th Century French novelist) stated, 'We don't receive wisdom; we must discover it for ourselves after a journey that no one can take for us or spare us.'

The physical journey could be local, in the same country, overseas or even in space, a place many science fiction texts take us. Fantasy writers create journeys of discovery in worlds of imagination and invention. Film also focuses on the concept of discovery through journey as we see in the range of road trip movies that seem so appealing to teen audiences. More serious films examine personal independence, the human condition and how one can discover something on the journey that will change or even save humanity. You will find many examples of this in film but try and choose something where the discovery has some significant personal and/or social impact and you can discuss techniques. Consider the idea of the journey as being inextricably linked to the concept of discovery as you make your way through the Area of Study.

Scientific and Technological Discovery

'Scientists have become the bearers of the torch of discovery in our quest for knowledge'

STEPHEN HAWKING

Regarding areas of discovery, foremost in many people's thoughts are the breakthroughs made in science and technology. They have immediate and significant impacts on modern day individuals and the way they interface with the world.

Examples of the impact of technology include:

- increased internet usage leading to the rise of social networking.
- miniaturisation of hand-held devices such as the iPad enabling people to communicate easily and more often.

- rapid changes in the way that data is stored such as the increased use of cloud-storage services has facilitated the development of much more flexible devices.

Einstein pointed out 'The process of scientific discovery is, in effect, a flight from wonder.' This is central to much of the debate that has raged over science in the past century or so. How do we progress scientifically and technologically and still maintain a moral and ethical basis? Should we chase many of the ideas that have arisen? For example the machines of war, the chemicals that kill and the genetic manipulations that can lead to social engineering are discoveries with ethical implications. Should there be limits and controls and if so how much? Discoveries can be fraught with danger on many levels.

While it is part of discovery to imagine and test the boundaries and seek new ways, it is also probably integral to human nature. With these new technologies the consequences are even greater than in the past as more people can be affected, more invasively and quickly. Dangers emerge as people discover new methods of being destructive, such as invading computers to distort programs with viruses or stealing through cybercrimes. These examples highlight that discoveries are not always positive.

Humanity must also grapple with the discovery of things such as climate change and environmental issues that are the result of industrialisation through discovered technologies. The consequences of many of the discoveries in the latter half of the last century are still being felt and new discoveries are needed to solve these problems. Discovery can be cyclical, inter-related and never-ending. Google '2014 Shift Happens' and watch a YouTube clip highlighting the rapid rate of discovery and change in this modern era!

Discovery as Creating New From Old

This is an intriguing idea probably best summed up in the idea of recycling materials to create something new. Old tyres can be used as soft fall for children's playgrounds, old ideas can be given new form, new ways can be thought up to approach a topic. Even just drawing attention to a common feature can enable people to discover something about it. This form of discovery is seen as creativity.

One example might be the light show Vivid which featured in Sydney. Prominent buildings such as the Opera House were illuminated with an exciting coloured light show. The buildings around the harbour foreshores were visible and bathed in psychedelic colours. People flocked to see the spectacle and the show received great reviews. The reactions evoked by the light show captured the idea of discovery and re-invention as otherwise familiar images were seen in an entirely new way. The sense of wonder and amazement experienced by young children observing the show was evidence of their discovery.

Sometimes a newly discovered thing can be as simple as reading a novel previously read or re-watching a film seen years before and getting something new or different from it. Great artists always borrow from the past and rearrange old elements into new discoveries for their audiences. Ideas such as this have led to new movements in the Arts or new methods of approaching a topic that casts new light on it. Postmodern texts such as the film *The Matrix,* use intertextuality as a key aspect.

Learning as Discovery

Learning in itself is a discovery that can make significant changes to an individual or a group. When we learn something that can be applied it is a small but potentially significant discovery for the individual or group. One significant piece of learning was the manipulation of fire, another the growing of crops, developing shelter and so on. While these are major discoveries other learning can be especially important for the individual. One example might be a breakthrough in reading or the ability to analyse and manipulate information to create something new. Consider this aspect of discovery as it can link to the other areas and be useful as an overriding idea to utilise as a thesis for the Area of Study essay.

Detection as Discovery

> *The basis of drama is... The struggle of the hero toward a specific goal at the end of which he realises that what kept him from it was, in the lesser drama, civilisation and, in the greater drama, the discovery of something that he did not set out to discover but which can be seen retrospectively as inevitable.*
>
> **DAVID MAMET**

The concept of detection as discovery is the integral aspect of the success of the eternally popular crime fiction genre and is also a major aspect of thrillers and similar literature, film and the visual arts. Paintings, for example, prove excellent material, to demonstrate how an individual can deduce something different from the same work as the person next to them. Detection, however, in its truest form is highly valued by audiences as it is about discovering the truth through clues.

Much literature has been written in this quest to make sense of a world where justice sometimes appears to be lacking. Of course the detective genre has changed much over the years and these variations have come to suit changing audiences and contexts but this search has rarely varied despite the form in which it is presented. Audiences love the sense of discovery in detection and an examination of any television or film guide will attest to the fact, as will an examination of library bookshelves.

"HOLMES GAVE ME A SKETCH OF THE EVENTS."

The Psychology of Discovery

'There'll always be serendipity involved in discovery'

JEFF BUZOS

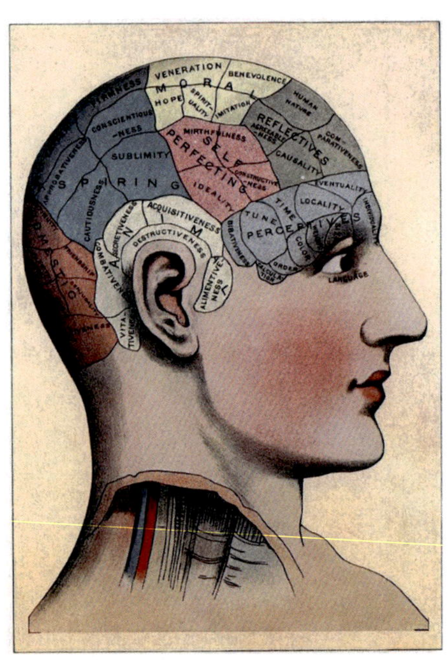

When I alluded to the innate need for discovery in the human psyche it wasn't superficial. The need for humanity to move ahead, to discover and to break boundaries is an important part of humanity's development and seems ingrained in us. The push to conquer new boundaries, to test, to push, to break boundaries is inherent in all development. Even if the discovery is the taste of a new food, the thrill of a new friend, or the discovery of any other sensory pleasure, it is a pleasure psychologically important to human development. The American writer Pearl S. Buck, who died in 1973, said that the basic discovery is the 'discovery of the relationship between men and women.' This is still true today. This quote could be used to explore the concept of discovery and to justify textual analysis from the perspective of feminist literary criticism. The field of Literary Criticism and new readings of texts is an example of boundary breaking.

There is something basic at an emotional level about discovery that attracts us to it. The new is important, broadening and thought provoking and this affects us on a psychological level. It is the emotional response that keeps people seeking the new, to discover and to absorb. This concept of the impact of discovery on our psyche is important as it is also a useful link to each of the texts and to your related material. It may be a useful concept to enable you to link your ideas together. Think about the basic psychological drives that motivate us and how they are important in all our discoveries.

Nationalism, Capitalism and other 'isms' as Drivers of Discovery

'People acting in their own self-interest is the fuel for all the discovery, innovation, and prosperity that powers the world'

JOHN STOSSEL

The idea that the 'isms' are drivers of discovery may not be appealing to some but there is no doubt that many of the discoveries of the last few centuries have been driven by them. One example is the race to land on the moon or the space race. This led to some awesome discoveries yet was driven by the great Cold War divide between the Communist Russian dictatorship and the American capitalist democratic system. Buoyed by the need to be first to set foot on the moon and discover what was there, billions were spent in making this happen.

Earlier still, the drive by nations such as Spain, Portugal and England to colonise the 'New World', particularly Africa and the Americas, led to many discoveries. National pride here was mixed with the drive for resources to support their ideology: religious, capitalist, communist or nationalist. This also led to many negatives such as exploitation in the race to conquer lands and spread 'civilisation'.

Capitalism, whatever your political belief, has been one of the greatest engines to drive discoveries over the centuries. This striving to produce product faster, more efficiently and thus, cheaply, has driven much innovation, prompted development of new technologies and resulted in new products. The instinct to improve and achieve is driven to its purest form by the capitalist system. It is not prudent here to discuss the pros and cons of the system itself but rather to recognise that it is a consummate motivator to Discovery. Gordon Gecko's quote from the film, *Wall Street*, sums up this philosophy brilliantly,

> *'Greed is right, greed works. Greed clarifies, cuts through and captures the essence of the evolutionary spirit. Greed in all of its forms; greed for life, for money, for love, knowledge has marked the upward surge of mankind.'*

Again relevant to this is the consideration of further analysing texts through the lens of literary criticism. For example, Marxist and New Historicist readings present different interpretations and may offer responders new insights and discoveries regarding texts.

Negative Aspects of Discovery

While it is common to have a positive image of discovery it is important to remember that it has negative aspects as well. For example, many of the early explorers who set out to discover new lands ended up dead. History is littered with such examples and many have gone down as glorious failures. One example is the story of Burke and Wills in Australia but you could also examine the exploration of the Antarctic and Arctic which have many failed expeditions. Other negatives can be found in the concept of discovering dreams of riches such as El Dorado or King Solomon's Mines.

The 'discovery' of new lands by European adventurers led to the exploitation of discovered natural resources. Indigenous peoples, considered uneducated savages, were often enslaved. The 'slave trade' was a negative by-product of this period of exploitation and discovery.

Away from this idea of exploration we can also have negatives in discoveries which yield promise such as nuclear power. This 'clean fuel' has been used for destructive purposes and Oppenheimer has said of his team's creation of the atomic bomb that it was a mistake. Many discoveries have been used negatively in war and in commerce for power and/or gain. We have even experienced psychological discoveries being used for brainwashing and other pernicious purposes. We have also mentioned the 'isms' that drive discovery and these can be negatively used as well. Communism killed millions and enslaved nations, patriotism in its extreme can lead to discovery but has impacted negatively on native populations and led to war.

Remember when you select a text for your related material or study a text there may be negatives to engage with that will enhance your understanding of the concept of discovery. Look for them to broaden your knowledge and ability to write clearly and formulate your own opinions.

Afterword on Discovery

'The pace of discovery is going unbelievably fast'

JAMES WATSON

Discovery is also about **possibility**, the idea that something in an imagination can be made real and attainable. Discovery is sometimes seeing the obvious and making use of it. Above all it entails faith/dreaming and an insatiable curiosity. When you read about many discoveries they are truly tales of failure with one success. Many stories tell of years of pain, toil, ridicule, dismal progress and rejection before success is achieved. Edison made a thousand bulbs before he got one to work. Failure is a constant with many people you will study in this topic until they discover their dream. They maintained their faith in the face of great adversity and this is what makes them discoverers. If it were easy everyone would do it!

Discoverers are also people who see what others have missed. Often they simply look at something in a new way. To look for new ideas, we must maintain an open mind. To discover for ourselves the mysteries of texts and how to unlock them, we must develop strategies for analysis and perseverance to achieve understanding.

Perhaps you think everything has been discovered as a pessimist might, but discoverers are optimists, people who continually seek success, or insight in achieving their goals or realising their dreams.

Questions for Discovery

- Define the term 'discovery' in your own words.
- How can discovery and possibility be connected?
- Discuss what the term discovery means to you.
- Create your own list of synonyms and antonyms for the word discovery. Then, choose two or three to use in your writing so the word discovery won't be repeated.
- Science is often connected with discovery. Research one such instance and write two paragraphs on it connecting it thematically to your set text.
- What is positive about discovery?
- Discuss the idea that discovery can be a two-edged sword.
- Discuss one discovery and the benefits of that discovery to humanity.
- Do you think the concept of discovery is integral to detective fiction? Explain your answer fully.
- Analyse one 'ism' and how discovery has been driven by it.
- Discuss some of the negatives associated with the concept of discovery.

STUDYING A NON-FICTION TEXT

The medium of a text is very important. If a text is non-fiction this means that its purpose is to report, reflect on or represent events, situations or trends. It is not created as a novel is; the composer does not choose the events of the story because the events have actually happened. Rather, the composer shapes the text by choosing which events to include and how he or she portrays them. The manner of this portrayal will depend on the composer's purpose. The composer adds his or her perspective to the description of the events. This bias will have an effect on the way the responder perceives the story. The responder can choose to accept, or reject the composer's **version** of events through a resistant reading.

Realism is created in a non-fiction text by the inclusion of actual people, events or situations. These may be reported objectively or subjectively.

Like the composers of fiction texts, the creator of a non-fiction text will create interest by the use of **techniques**. These are the elements of the text which are manipulated by the composer to present their ideas effectively. When you are discussing how the composer represents his ideas, you MUST discuss techniques. Language techniques are sometimes referred to as **stylistic devices**.

The language techniques used in non-fiction often overlap those used in fiction.

STUDYING A DOCUMENTARY

A documentary according to dictionary.com is:

> *a television show or film based on recreating an actual event, life story, era etc. that purports to be factually accurate and contains no fictional content.*

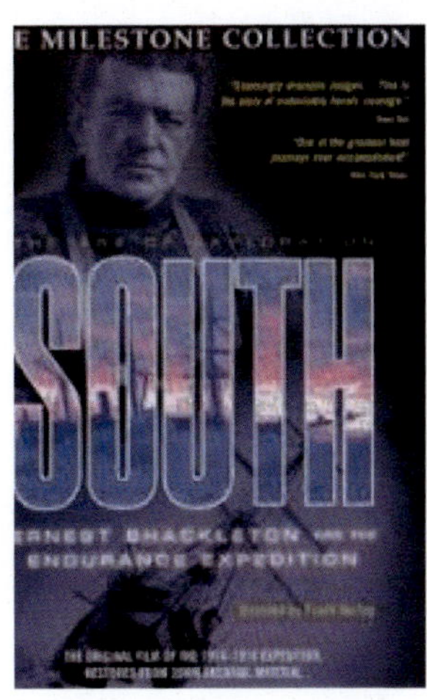

The documentary form has the concept of informing the audience of a 'real life' situation but you will note that the word 'purports' comes into the definition above. A documentary inherently has biases based on the beliefs of the producer/ director even if they don't intentionally set out to project one particular point of view. The documentary deals with fact and is based on real life situations but at the core of a documentary is the need to touch the audience and call them to action. The purpose is to inform and to also inspire inner or social change. A documentary might/should inspire change and this is where the different techniques involved in making a documentary assume relevance.

A documentary will have an initial script that has to be adaptable. As when you film real life situations, flexibility is the key to enabling the audience to experience what the subject(s) are experiencing. This experience may/should evolve as the filming occurs. While the balance has shifted from pure information to information and entertainment, the focus must still be on the subject.

There is no specific formal structure or formula for composing a documentary and they are all structured very differently, often depending on the subject. For example if they are about a person the footage will be focused on that individual but if it is a more amorphous subject such as climate change the challenges are very different for the producers. Documentaries can call on a variety of people and techniques to make their case. These include;

- Experts such as professors, politicians, etc depending on the subject
- Statistics
- Interviews
- On location shots
- Commentary i.e. voiceover
- Anecdotes, stories
- Graphs and charts
- Recounts and descriptions
- Dramatisations and Re-creations
- Use of colour, black and white, animation
- Archival footage
- Montages
- Music, silences, sound
- Panel discussions with/without an audience

These are a few examples but you also need to consider the style of the documentary. For example older style classical documentaries are very rigidly chronological, factual and focused on dramatised realism. This has morphed into a more docu-drama style over the years and now audiences expect entertainment with their information. For most documentaries, extensive research is required so that the content is factual and verifiable. Even in documentaries such as *The Man Who Made History* which is based on one man, the details have been researched and the content made accessible to the audience.

Research ensures that the audience gets to see the heart of the issue, the part that is engaging, interesting and ultimately unique to that subject. A good documentary will establish a 'hook' to keep viewers interested, then establish the core assertion of the subject. It arouses curiosity in the audience and gives hope of some change with action or change of ideas. Much like a fiction text, a documentary may also have a strong narrative, a protagonist, characters and a conclusion. You can use some techniques, from your knowledge of fiction, just be alert to the subtle differences in purposes of the genres. In the documentary you can also have a backstory, points of view and conflict which engenders emotions. It is the emotional engagement with the subject that creates empathy with the audience. We will examine how this is achieved in *The Man Who Made History* later in this guide.

It is also important to link these ideas related to form, with your Area of Study, Discovery. Nasht's documentary, due to its infomative style, helps viewers discover Hurley and his work. Through Hurley's work we vicariously discover places and people of different contexts. We learn our discoveries are manipulated through composers' choices. Both Hurley and Nasht's artistic legacies, seen here, are results of 'deliberate and careful planning.' They are also evoked by,'curiosity, necessity and wonder.'

THE WRITER/ DIRECTOR – SIMON NASHT

Simon Nasht is a producer and director who is a well-known filmmaker in Australian media. He has worked for the Australian Broadcasting Commission and the documentaries he has completed for them include *The Bridge, Addicted to Money, How Kevin Bacon Cured Cancer* and *Dick Smith's Population Puzzle*.

In 2010 he began a joint venture with Dick Smith called Smith & Nasht. The website tells us,

> ***Smith&Nasht*** *is a new Australian media venture formed as a creative partnership between philanthropist and entrepreneur Dick Smith and filmmaker Simon Nasht. Our projects stem from true stories, and we find the best way to present them to the world through documentary, drama and transmedia experiences.*
>
> *We're currently producing and developing a wide range of projects for the global market including documentaries, feature films and online games for social change. Our partners include leading producers, broadcasters, foundations and social action groups around the world.*
>
> *Managing director and founder Simon Nasht has 25 years' experience as a leading international filmmaker in Australia, the UK and the US and has consistently produced high-rating and award-winning documentaries for broadcasters including the ABC, SBS, BBC, Channel 4, ITV, PBS, Discovery, National Geographic, ZDF, NHK and RAI. He has run successful production companies in London and New York and has worked as a foreign correspondent, political reporter and is a best-selling author.*

HTTP://SMITHANDNASHT.COM/ABOUT/

CONTEXT

The career and life of Hurley (1885–1962) spanned a very turbulent era in Australian history. Hurley lived through the Depression, both World Wars, post war immigration and the modernisation of Australian society. It was an exciting time to be an adventurer and explorer as it was a time before mass communication, easy plane travel and Google Earth.

Raised in Glebe, Hurley ran away at age thirteen to work at the Lithgow steel mill and bought his first camera at seventeen. A self-taught man, Hurley moved on from still photography to help create the documentary and then on to dramatic feature films. His documentary *Sagebrush and Silver* (1941) was nominated for an Academy Award. It is important to remember that the context of Hurley's work was a very different world to the one you live in. People hadn't seen any of the places or events he was filming. Australia was a far more isolated place and he gave people a sense of adventure and an insight into unknown places and worlds.

While Hurley's sense of the dramatic seems naïve in the modern world, his ability to capture images and develop narratives around them is still valuable. While many of his images are adapted and manipulated to suit the circumstances he wished to create, they still provide insights into the world he knew and the world as it once was. Hurley's images of Australia, for example, are still used in books and brochures as he captured the essence of the Australian landscape in his final period of creativity.

Hurley's works have become extremely valuable and are held in collections all over the world including the Royal Geographic Society, the Australian War Memorial and the Scott Polar Research

Institute. As you study the documentary, *Frank Hurley - The Man Who Made History* by Simon Nasht, keep in mind the world he lived in and the context of his work. Think about who he was working for and how it affected his portrayal of events.

Frank Hurley is a significant figure in Australian social and cultural history. As you shall discover in the documentary he was also a controversial figure in Australian history. You will need to decide what your position is on Hurley and his work and it is important to come to your own conclusions.

DOCUMENTARY ANALYSIS

Introductory Notes

Frank Hurley - The Man Who Made History by writer/director Simon Nasht is a documentary about the man who invented the genre. It is about how he collected news, exciting news and made it into a subjective adventure rather than an objective analysis of events. More on this aspect later. The main focus of the Area of Study is, of course, discovery and there is plenty to cover in this text. There were the physical discoveries that Hurley made on his adventures, the artistic discoveries he made but also our own discoveries. Additionally, Hurley gave people a vision of Australia that allowed them to discover our country. Nasht made his own discoveries which prompted his choices in the documentary.

This guide will focus on each of the sections in the documentary and approach them as separate entities for the sake of analysis. You should approach your own studies a little more holistically at first and then select, as I will, specific sets of evidence to support your ideas on discovery and discovering. Each chapter selection will have a a summary of the contents, examples from that chapter on discovery and some analysis of the techniques used to convey information and the aspect of discovery. You should read the section on the documentary genre before proceeding with the next sections.

Frank Hurley - The Man Who Made History has much to offer in our study of discovery and it is an intriguing examination of Australia's past as well as the man. I hope you enjoy tracing Hurley's life and work and viewing his enduring, striking images. For a closer examination of these images and some historical data have a look at the selection in the photo gallery available on the DVD. These graphics are all in the DVD but the stills allow you to appreciate the way Hurley discovered images that others could not see. They also demonstrate the way Hurley discovered new ways to create the images he desired.

"Endurance in Antarctica, 1915 Hurley a090007" by Frank Hurley - State Library of NSW. Licensed under Public Domain via Wikimedia Commons - http://commons.wikimedia.org/wiki/File:Endurance_in_Antarctica,_1915_Hurley_a090007.jpg#mediaviewer/File:Endurance_in_Antarctica,_1915_Hurley_a090007.jpg

Mawson Expedition

This chapter covers the complete Mawson expedition that left Tasmania in 1911 and where Hurley initially made his name as a photographer. Note the use of original, archival footage cut into the script to engage the audience and show Hurley's work. Remember that it is said later that Hurley had to tell a story and this is also true of Nasht so think, as you watch, how both men do this. One obvious clue is the chronology but also Nasht follows the career, not just the life as we can detect from the headings.

Mawson's journey began when Hurley was twenty-six and Hurley remembered it well. An interview frames the work as he tells of his life in Lithgow. Hurley was 'working class' while the others were university educated but he was resourceful. We learn this from his biographer who is used frequently to link sections. Also here at 1:24 the split screen is used to link the two eras. Similarly, contrast is applied effectively so we can discover that much has changed in the harsh Antarctic conditions. This is the journey that made Hurley as a photographer and on which he discovered his calling. Here he found his 'real work' and 'undiscovered portals'. His work, *Argonauts of the South,*is like a hero's journey but there were hardships and the heavy camera became a problem. (A Hero's Journey is a model seen in storytelling. It was proposed by Joseph Campbell in 1949 and traces common steps of a hero's journey From Call to Adventure through to Return. You can search to term, Monomyth or Hero's Journey to find out more details). At this stage of the documentary we see shots of 'Home of the Blizzard' as Hurley is seen to discover the windiest place on earth, Commonwealth Bay. In turn, we, as viewers, discover the place vicariously.

Here the blizzard became the story and we get the voiceover describing how he came to discover the sense of story before Joanna Wright of the Royal Geographic Society tells us how he married the story to the images. She says it was a 'seminal moment' as it was the first time this had been done. The sense of the hero's journey was repeated throughout his life. Images of Mawson's expedition give us a sense of the hardship endured.

The human stories related about Hurley and the other men gives us the human aspect and we learn of Hurley's humour and strong work ethic. In his darkroom he inscribed the words 'Near enough is not good enough' and this sums up his life and work.

Next we are introduced to Hurley's daughters, Adelie and Toni who elaborate on his work and background. They discuss him as a father and we see them set in the Antarctic to show their sense of adventure. Once you get past the concept of them wearing the same outfits, what they say is a great insight into their father. It allows us to discover the man not just the image he portrayed. They are very loyal to a father they barely saw which shows his work ethic, aura and drive. They are 'guardians of his legacy' and we see how he lived his adventures 'not just photographed them'. Note here the use of reconstructed scenes – a common documentary technique in modern works, to elaborate on the words – as we see the three men trudge through the snow.

Questions for Mawson Expedition

- Why was Hurley the odd man out on the expedition?
- What does Hurley tells us about himself in this initial interview?
- Describe the problems Hurley faced on the journey.
- Analyse, using two specific quotes, what Hurley discovers about himself on this journey.
- Discuss one technique Hurley discovers on this journey.

Examine the graphics. What do these images conjure in your mind? Imagine how the early explorers might have felt when confronted by this landscape. (http://commons.wikimedia.org/wiki/File%3AAntarctica_wind_Mawson_Hurley.jpg by Frank Hurley (National Library of Australia) [Public domain], via Wikimedia Commons).

Shackleton Expedition

The scene cuts to London 1914. Hurley goes back with Shackleton's Antarctic expedition to make 'his fortune'. He got part ownership of the photos and the journey becomes a wonderful 'epic' as Hurley had the images to go with the story.

The *Endurance* became trapped in the icy sea and we have amazing pictures as it was both freed and then crushed by the ice. These are stark, intriguing images, especially the night shot where the boat is lit by magnesium flares. Hurley used images to create drama and many of these were 'elaborately constructed'. The visuals he took make the Shackleton trip accessible to viewers and we learn how hard he worked to keep some of the film, just to retain the historic images. Hurley would not 'give up his precious negatives', even sacrificing food in order to retain this evidence.

Eventually the party landed at Elephant Rock where Hurley manufactured one of the most controversial of his images. Shackleton left the Rock and Hurley manipulated the photo to create drama. It is a superb photo but not an authentic, natural image. The men survived many hardships until Shackleton miraculously returned. Hurley claimed the photo of his return was real but it was a shot of Shackleton leaving. It is a 'different truth' and now these photos have 'transcended art and history' and the plates have become artefacts themselves.

On this journey Hurley discovered how to build on his reputation, both as an explorer/adventurer but also as an artist who tells a story. For him, his art was about discovering the perfect image, regardless of whether the composition was natural. Hurley's work confirms him as a storyteller, not an objective photographer, and we discover this as Nasht shows viewers how Hurley manipulated images. The interviews support this viewpoint and we have to decide whether the manipulations are truthful and whether the objective story is more important. That is something viewers need to discover for themselves.

Questions for Shackleton Expedition

- Why was the Shackleton expedition of particular importance to Hurley?
- Discuss Hurley's manipulation of the expedition photos. Do you agree with Hurley's analysis that they should be dramatic?
- Describe Hurley's reaction to losing his plates off *The Endurance.* How do we see him the respond to his surviving film?
- Analyse, using two specific quotes, what Hurley discovers about himself on the Shackleton expedition.
- Is it important to the story that Nasht shows us how these manipulations are achieved?

WWI – Europe

Hurley was a cameraman on the Western Front and we see footage of Flanders in 1917. His initial shots were part of the heroic story but, 'they began to change' as the reality set in. The war context is a stark contrast to the Antarctic where human life is precious. He sees mutilated bodies and wonders at the murder. The photos here are shocking and are designed to show the horrors of war. Extracts from his diaries are read. Then, he begins to use colour to illustrate further the reality of war. It was the first time colour had been used this way.

The shot cuts to the Australian War Memorial present day where Stephen Burton, senior photographer, shows viewers how Hurley manipulated the plates to get colour. Even with colour, Hurley felt 'something was missing' and there 'was a gulf between what he saw and what was on the glass plates.' Curator, Ian Affleck, says Hurley decided to 'make photographs' which he did by combining various images into a dramatic picture. This leads him into 'bitter conflict' with official war historian Charles Bean who said these manipulations were 'fakes' and demanded they be stopped. Bean wanted the 'literal truth' whereas Hurley was all about the images. Dr Martin Jolly says 'on one level the photos were fakes,' but he also comments, they were a 'phantasmagoric mixture' that became a 'modern spectacle'. Affleck isn't as impressed and says these manipulations have 'undermined their historic value'. He thinks 'Bean is right' and the authentic action is missed'.

Hurley defended his images and even resigned due to the controversy over constructed images but he was eventually allowed to exhibit some of the pictures.

The documentary then cuts to Ypres in Belgium where viewers learn 40,000 Australians were killed in four months but 'he gave a face to their names'. In this chapter we discover Hurley's passion for his work and the lengths he would go to get the shot he wanted. We discover the controversy around this idea, we get different perspectives and we also discover something about history itself. Note here the use of interviews with modern commentators interspersed with readings from the events at the time to build these ideas. Think also about how Nasht allows us to make up our own minds regarding our opinion of Hurley's manipulations. Can the recording of any event be totally objective? What are you discovering about the nature of History and aspects of subjectivity and objectivity?

Questions for WWI – Europe

- Discuss how Hurley's attitude to life changed because of his exposure to the war.
- Analyse the argument that Bean had with Hurley over the manipulation of photos. What was the outcome?
- Using comments from Affleck and Jolly analyse why the argument continues into the modern era.
- How does this chapter of the documentary show Hurley's passion for his work?
- Is it important to the narrative line that Nasht allows us to consider what position we hold on Hurley's work? Do you think there is any bias in the documentary? Discuss with reference to your own discoveries about Hurley's work and the world.

WWI – Middle East

Hurley was reassigned to Palestine and he made the Light Horse the focus of his work. Most of the real fighting was over so he recreated war activities, 'it was no longer war photography, it was an epic circus with Hurley as the ringmaster'. He used some of the footage in his movie *40,000 Horsemen* (1940), most of which was filmed on a Sydney beach. He is now described as, 'the master of illusion.'

We see shots of his diary and are told entries are missing from March 1918 when he met and married, in a whirlwind romance, opera singer, Antoinette Rosalind Leighton. Their twin daughters relate the story of their mother and father's courtship which included a brief holiday on the Nile. It was the only holiday they had together in forty two years. The twins tell how their father was always away. This short chapter tells us about how he began to try to create an image of himself and a little more about the person rather than the photographer.

Questions for WWI – Middle-East

- Discuss the impact of Hurley's footage in the modern era.
- Analyse the romance and marriage to Antoinette. Why do you think he married and then basically abandoned his family?
- Using evidence from the documentary, how do you see Hurley at this stage in your text? Has your view changed?

Papua

Hurley, after the war, saw a market for 'exciting adventure films' and chose New Guinea which was then unexplored and had 'wonderful imagery'. Note again how the split screen links the two eras as we enter New Guinea and see it as a place where Hurley tried to build his new career.

Now Hurley becomes the main focus of his own art. It was a major expedition although it did have a 'veneer' of science with a biologist, but it was primarily about Hurley. He wanted to make his name and he engineered events and excitement including allusions to cannibalism. Again, the modern becomes interspersed with the historical footage. In their search for excitement and plunder, Hurley's party was 'unscrupulous' and ran afoul of the authorities with their 'sensational aims'. The publicity over this was used by Hurley to build even more excitement but the biologist with him, McCulloch, said they did steal things. McCulloch's career never survived the scandal and two years later he suicided.

Hurley, however, 'turned the fiasco into a triumph'. The film he made, *Pearls and Savages*, toured the world. It was sensational and when he didn't succeed in America he marketed the film as a 'Lost Tribe' which caught attention. He was then backed to make two 'steamy melodramas' in New Guinea by a British company. The resultant stories and silent films had no popular appeal. The films were heavily criticised and they died a quiet death at the box office.

Hurley did nothing constructive at the time for Papuan culture, but he did leave footage of their heritage which has helped rebuild it. This chapter is not a positive portrayal of Hurley and his discovery of these peoples had a very negative effect on them in terms of cultural loss.

By Frank Hurley (Life time: 1962) [Public domain], via Wikimedia Commons

Questions for Papua

- Discuss how Hurley attempted to change his image by exploring New Guinea.
- Why was Hurley described as 'unscrupulous'?
- Why does Nasht include the story of McCulloch?
- How does this section of *Frank Hurley – The Man Who Made History* show Hurley's ability to be the showman rather than an historian or photographer?
- Why does Nasht include Hurley's failure as a feature film maker of melodramas? What does it allow us to discover about Hurley?
- Do you think Nasht criticises Hurley for his pillage of the local culture? Use evidence from the documentary to support your ideas.
- Which is the one benefit Hurley left the Indigenous tribes?

Banzare Expedition

Hurley agrees to go back to the Antarctic but there was no great story with this expedition. He films much on the beach near Sydney and adds sound on his return to try and compete with the talkies. This section shows Hurley becoming more desperate to be relevant in the modern world and his manipulations become even more excessive. We need to consider here if the time and tone of the narration is changing. Compare it with the early analysis of Hurley. Consider how the phrasing has changed and look for inherent criticisms of the man (think of the comments about him leaving Antoinette for the Antarctic and not telling her).

This chapter is very brief as the Banzare Expedition appears to be a failure, with no real redeeming features in the cinematography or content. As always though, Hurley reinvents himself and discovers a new career.

Questions for Banzare

- Analyse why this expedition failed to enhance Hurley's career?
- Why was Hurley desperate to be still seen as relevant in the more modern era?
- What additional information do we discover about Hurley?

State Library of New South Wales [Public domain or CC BY-SA 3.0 au (http://creativecommons.org/licenses/by-sa/3.0/au/deed.en)], via Wikimedia Commons

Cinesound Studios

Hurley's 'dream of conquering the world' faded and he got a job at Cinesound Studios as head cameraman. He made epic, 'escapist' films about Australia and he excelled at this 'propagandistic' cinema. He did not like the studio system and returned to making travelogues which were sponsored by the government and which were faithful to the values of that government led by Joseph Lyons. *Oasis* (1936),a film about Aboriginal culture, is seen as extremely patronising today. When evaluated in the context of production, however, it reflected the beliefs and values of the era. Hurley found his usual mythical story and he used the national story in films such as *A Nation is Built* (1938) which extol the virtues of the nation.

These propagandist films suited Hurley whose cinema and methodology were able to manipulate images to suit the perception he was trying to create. It is important here to note that Hurley also re-discovered himself many times throughout his career and was able to show that discovery was also about adapting to changing circumstances. These discoveries may be acceptable and useful, even dramatic at one particular time but irrelevant at others. Hurley was about to re-invent himself again as another war beckoned.

Questions for Cinesound Studios

- Why did Hurley leave Cinesound?
- Discuss why the propaganda style of film suited the manipulations of Hurley's style?
- Discuss one discovery in this chapter which was exciting in its context but which is now seen as irrelevant.

WWII

We begin by seeing footage of *Drive into Libya* (1941). Hurley was desperate to be part of the filming. He resorted to faking again and the footage looks contrived. We discover how Hurley faked the photographs and how it caused some disquiet amongst the troops who saw him, taking liberties 'with heroism.' The narrator then states 'the magician had run out of tricks' and Hurley became a 'lonely man' who became 'weary'.

Despite his inadequate efforts, the British recruit him to make movies to 'bolster' the weakening hold they had in the region. In *Cradle of Civilisation* (1946), Hurley uses his skills of manipulation to create a film that shows harmony in the Middle East. This was no mean feat even then. His type of footage and base propaganda is Hurley striving to remain relevant but it is not lasting footage or images, unlike his early work. After six years he returned to Australia.

Questions for WWII

- Describe why Hurley resorted to desperate faking. Why did it cause consternation amongst the troops?
- Discuss why *Cradle of Civilisation* (1946) is considered propaganda?
- Note here the varying nature of discovery. Hurley's manipulation of events results in products which were regarded very differently in different contexts. Analyse one example.

An example of Hurley's manipulated images from World War One

State Library of New South Wales [CC BY-SA 3.0 au (http://creativecommons.org/licenses/by-sa/3.0/au/deed.en)], via Wikimedia Commons

http://commons.wikimedia.org/wiki/File%3AEpisode_after_Battle_of_Zonnebeke_1918_Hurley.jpg

Australia

In an interview his daughters state that Hurley returned to a different world. Adelie had become the first female press photographer but the real shock was that the family was in financial difficulty. Hurley reinvents himself again at sixty-one. He returns to his roots as a scenic photographer and Gael Newton of the National Gallery of Australia said he was, 'the face of scenic portraiture until his death'.

Hurley's work was seen everywhere and his work was extremely popular. His view was a 'very endorsed' picture of Australia according to Newton. His work showed the nation as 'he wished it to be' with no Aboriginals, poor or migrants. The author, David Malouf, says they are manipulated images and the reality was not the same. This is the story of his work and possibly the narrative of his life.

Hurley managed to rebuild the family fortune before his death at seventy six. On his death his wife gave away his cameras and spent her inheritance. The conclusion to the documentary points out that in a 'world searching for heroes' Hurley's work is again popular. He made no apologies for his manipulations and he said that the 'camera was a piece of mechanical apparatus, you are its intellect'.

Questions for Australia

- What conclusions have the twins come to about their father over the course of *Frank Hurley - The Man Who Made History* ?
- Discuss why Hurley was successful at scenic photography?
- Why might Hurley's work have become popular once again or re-discovered?
- Why does Nasht choose to show the auction room scenes to bookend the documentary?

http://commons.wikimedia.org/wiki/File%3AA_radiant_turret_lit_by_the_midsummer_midnight_sun.jpg By State Library of New South Wales from Australia [Public domain], via Wikimedia Commons

DOCUMENTARY QUESTIONS AND ACTIVITIES

- In one paragraph state the purpose of this documentary.
- Does *Frank Hurley – The Man Who Made History* give a fair representation of the man? Discuss your response with direct reference to the content of the documentary.
- Why might Nasht have used *Frank Hurley – The Man Who Made History* as the title for the documentary? How relevant and appropriate do you think the title is to the concept of Discovery?
- What did Hurley discover about himself on the first journey with Mawson?
- The Mawson journey also allowed Hurley to discover the value of the narrative in documentary. What story did he tell? How did this affect his later work?
- Discuss the use of image manipulation during the Shackleton expedition. How did the discovery of this technique affect his later career?
- What conflict did Hurley have with Charles Bean during World War One?
- Do you think Hurley's manipulated images are more effective than the reality? Explain your response.
- Explain how Papua is a turning point in Hurley's career.
- Why is Hurley criticised for his Papuan journey?
- Hurley the 'showman' is evident in his marketing of the Papuan film in America. How does he become described as the 'showman' rather than an historian or photographer?
- Using Papua as your evidence, discuss how discovery can also be seen as conquest.
- Discuss the description of Hurley as an adventurer. Do you think the description is apt?
- Analyse and support the idea that Hurley's twin

daughters are also on a journey of discovery to find their father.

- Why was Hurley less successful in capturing images, both still and on film, in World War Two?
- Using the documentaries *A Nation is Built* (1938) and *Cradle of Civilisation* (1946) discuss how Hurley's style suits propaganda film. Use specific shots and ideas to support your opinion.
- Hurley is described as an outdoors type of man. Is this true?
- Why was Hurley less successful in his attempts at fictional movies such as the melodramas he shot in Papua?
- Describe Hurley's final career re-invention as a scenic photographer. Why was he so successful at this? What criticisms have been made of this section of his career?

"Endurance Final Sinking" by Royal Geographic Society - http://indigo.ie/~jshack/Other%20 Ernest%20Pages/endurance.html. Licensed under Public Domain via Wikimedia Commons - http://commons.wikimedia.org/wiki/File:Endurance_Final_Sinking.jpg#mediaviewer/File:Endurance_Final_Sinking.jpg

SETTING

Frank Hurley - The Man Who Made History covers an inordinate number of wonderful settings that range from the icy Antarctic to the steamy jungles of Papua, the beaches of Sydney and the European capitals. What is important isn't necessarily the settings themselves but the impact they had on Hurley's work. The structure of your text, the documentary, reflects this.

When we examine setting, it is Hurley's interaction with it that is our interest and this is seen in the images and cinematography he created. Whether the image is manipulated by Hurley or not, the fascinating places he ventured into and some he helped discover, are what makes his work unique and intriguing. This is especially so if we consider the context of when he shot his work.

The world was a very different place then. Hurley showed Australians and gave Australians, and later the world, a taste of adventure and a sense of discovery that they might not have gained elsewhere. In reality, Hurley did risk his life to get shots and he was in dangerous settings. Dubbed the 'mad photographer' Hurley always put his art first and sought out dangerous settings throughout his career. He even travelled outback Australia late in his life to get the scenic shots that revitalised his career.

When we examine setting in terms of discovery we can see that place is integral to Hurley's work. The settings provide the enduring images that still capture the attention of audiences. This is seen in the auction, the interest in his work and the way he is spoken about by some of the experts in the documentary. Indeed some of the settings are still complex and difficult to get to, capturing the imagination of modern audiences.

The Antarctic, for example, is not a place many have visited and climatic conditions there are changing rapidly. It is place where the hardships he filmed and the stories he created around his images still engender respect from modern audiences. Despite changes to weather, snow and ice, the place has not been affected by global commercial imperatives.

In other places such as Papua, Hurley has left a different kind of legacy. There, time and context have not been so kind to Hurley or his work. While the images still resonate, his 'unscrupulous' behaviour in his treatment of the Indigenous peoples was, and is, unacceptable.

Setting plays an important role in the discovery process during *Frank Hurley - The Man Who Made History* and it needs to be considered in any analysis. How has Nasht foregrounded its importance?

http://commons.wikimedia.org/wiki/File%3AElephant_island_party.jpg. By Frank Hurley [Public domain], via Wikimedia Commons

Setting Questions and Activities

- What role does setting play in the initial achievements of Hurley?
- Why might the settings that his work encapsulated play an important role in the relevance of his work for future contexts?
- Discuss one setting Hurley visited in his lifetime and why that setting might have captured the attention of audiences at the time.
- Analyse one setting in terms of what Hurley discovered about the setting and himself.
- On the Internet, search images for one setting that Hurley shot or filmed during his career. Examine some of the images and discuss how they are portrayed. Then, compare them to Hurley's work. Discuss any differences you see in the portrayals. What do you discover about how Hurley's eye and imagination affect setting?
- Find one of the settings Hurley shot such as Belgium, Israel, Papua New Guinea on Google Earth. What type of country is it? Why would it be a place of discovery for Hurley and his audiences?

MAIN IDEA – REVIEW

Discovery and Discoveries

Always keep the rubric for Area of Study – Discovery, in mind.

The first aspect to consider is physical discovery. What are the physical discoveries Hurley makes over his career? These comprise the places and we have read about them in the settings. These physical discoveries are full of excitement and Hurley emphasises this excitement by his manipulation of images and the story creation he imposes on them. The concept of the 'hero's journey' is re-emphasised in all aspects of his work and allows the audience to discover the place, Hurley's work and perhaps something about themselves.

The concept of discovery as conquest is also conveyed in the documentary. This is emphasised in the shots of men claiming the land for King and country but also in images of war. Perhaps the idea of conquest also comes into mind when we consider Hurley's trip into Papua. While this is not a war-like conquest it is a cultural conquest and highlights the destruction of Indigenous cultures by colonial rulers and religious evangelists.

While we may not agree with war or colonisation we can see that it is exciting and intriguing for audiences once removed and Hurley captures that excitement and sense of 'man' overcoming great odds to succeed and/or survive. This links back to the sense of the hero's journey and the search people have for that kind of story. These stories are found in the kind of adventures and discoveries Hurley covered in his career. Even later in his career, back in Australia, Hurley made stories that fitted this ethos despite the fact that they might not have been a realistic portrayal of the nation. Hurley's search for stories, for narrative, is what people liked and sought.

Another idea you might consider is the way that Hurley's twin daughters discover their father and the heritage he left them. The discoveries they make about their father contribute to their knowledge of him and build a deeper picture of the man. They admit they did not see their father often as he was always absent and he was a bit of a mystery to them. Their search was about finding him as a person and a father and so they visit many of the places he did and we see them in Antarctica. They become emotional when they see Elephant Rock. Consider what they discover and also how they view their mother.

Another aspect of discovery is that of discovering the truth in Hurley's work and the places he portrayed. Much of *Frank Hurley – The Man Who Made History* is about the issue of truth in art and how Hurley manipulated images to create narratives rather than provide objective pictorial records of material and events. The argument between Hurley and Bean is a solid example of the issue and it is clearly enunciated in the arguments given over the WWI pictures he changed in the darkroom. This argument still evokes discussion today and Hurley has detractors and admirers and both are given voice in the documentary. One discovery you make as you view is how these images were modified and you, personally, need to decide how you view these changes. Was Hurley opportunistic, ethically challenged or morally corrupt? How are judgements affected by contextual value systems?

Another aspect you need to consider when viewing the documentary is whether Hurley was an artist or historian. He considers himself a showman so I think the evidence highlighted by Nasht leans towards the concept of Hurley as an artist portraying how he saw the world rather than the reality of the world he experienced. We see how Hurley is often vague about the truth, even in his portrayal of Australia during his time after WWII. We need to place this in context and remember who commissioned his work. Often it was a government agency and his work had a specific purpose as in Palestine. We need to consider the fact that while Hurley's work is, and has been used for historical purposes, it isn't necessarily a factual record and is subjective. The composer's purpose and the intended audience of his work is key here.

In considering this aspect we may also think about how discovery can be viewed positively or negatively. The negative aspects of discovery can be seen in the effect of Hurley's work in Papua when the Indigenous peoples were adversely affected by his very intrusive excursion into their midst. The impact of his visit can be seen in the documentary through how the local people reflect on the loss of culture, not just by Hurley's party who stole artefacts but by those who followed. This is an interesting aspect of discovery in a colonial era and one that may be a useful link to your choice of related material.

Finally we can look at the further representations of discovery and discoveries and how they are portrayed in *Frank Hurley – The Man Who Made History*. The documentary helps us discover the work of Hurley and through his work, we can vicariously discover places. We will examine this in the next section.

http://commons.wikimedia.org/wiki/File%3AA_trench_in_the_low_flat_country_near_La_Bassee_Ville_(3007144955).jpg By National Media Museum from UK [see page for license], via Wikimedia Commons

TECHNIQUES

Documentary Techniques

It is through techniques that aspects relating to Discovery are revealed. The documentary helps viewers discover Hurley and his work. Through his images we also, vicariously, discover places. Nasht's documentary, like the images of Hurley and his work, highlights how responders can be led and manipulated by the choices composers make. Both Nasht and Hurley's work is a result of, 'deliberate and careful planning'. The selection of techniques emphasises this. The work of the documentary maker is, 'creative, intellectual'. It is a result of, 'curiosity or...wonder'. These quotes are taken from the rubric and are worth reflecting on as they relate to discovery.

The techniques used in a documentary are designed to create emotional pertinence and control over an audience. To do this the director and his team have to 'show not tell' with pictures and allow the audience to find their way. To assist this process a narration is often used. The narration must be relevant, simple and linked to the visuals. Usually, narration is either a first person or third person omniscient narrator sometimes referred to as the 'voice of God'. *Frank Hurley – The Man Who Made History* employs a third person narrator. The narration is emotive in parts and slightly judgemental at times for what may be expected to be a detached, omniscient narrator.

Also, when you watch the documentary think about the 'set-up'. In this instance, it is the conflict over Hurley's work and his manipulation of images. This is where the tension is created through the idea and counter-idea. In *Frank Hurley – The Man*

Who Made History the idea is based around the enduring value of Hurley's work and its relevance to historians. Here we get arguments from several perspectives, both historical and contemporary. Evidence is garnered from a variety of sources, especially interviews from 'experts'. Here we have discoveries influenced by,' the perspectives of the individual and others.'

This choice of material raises the question of what is included by a director. A director has control of shots, scenes and the work itself. Obviously, conflict is better television and it is the thing that drives the documentary. Yet, it is also about the man and not just the work and Nasht gives, along with the analysis of the work, an overview of Hurley's life. This comes through in the sections with his daughters and the information we are given about the wife. We only get glimpses of this as his family were a minor part of his life and the commentary and amount of time they are given reflects this.

The issue of bias must be mentioned and while Nasht explores this in the sense of Hurley's work we also need to be critical of Nasht in regard to this. When you watch the documentary think about what he includes and what he wants the audience to see. Obviously much about the man's life has been omitted and particular aspects chosen to focus on. Think about why Nasht has arranged the work in the manner he has and what effect this has on the presentation and reception of material.

The final decision must lie with you, the viewer, and it is important to consider what Nasht reveals and what you discover as a viewer or what we discover, collectively as an audience. 'The widely-held assumptions and beliefs about aspects of human experience and the world' will shape your conclusions. The main concern in analysing the text itself, is how documentary techniques show discovery and support the ideas in the text. Look for specific examples of how discoveries are presented. For example, Nasht allows us to discover how Hurley manipulated images in the darkroom. We discover Hurley's passion for his work, we see his daughters search to discover their father. You need to decide what Nasht presents, what he allows us to discover and whether it is balanced. *Frank Hurley – The Man Who Made History* is generally balanced in its approach in my opinion and includes both criticisms and praise both for the man and his work.

In technical terms Nasht uses a variety of techniques to engage the audience. He uses long shots and long-wide shots to orientate the audience to particular unfamiliar locations. This is more so in the foreign locations but he also does this with the Australian scenes as the audience is not necessarily Australian as Hurley is well-known internationally. It is clever direction to give orientation, especially as many of the locations are shot by Hurley himself and are difficult to get to and in some cases cannot be shot now as the setting has been lost. Nasht also uses a split screen technique to unite the different eras and establish a context for the information and shots that follow. He sets the scene, then the narrator will provide information/commentary and then an expert will fill in the more complex details or we will be given an example of the work or both. In addition to camera angles, the structure of the work helps to distinguish the various settings and to highlight their importance.

Another choice that Nasht makes is to use much of Hurley's material to illustrate the ideas he is conveying. Through Hurley's work we discover much about the man and we see first-hand how the quote 'Near enough is not good enough' applies directly to what he set out to achieve. It is this thread that runs through the documentary and is the backdrop to his striving to achieve the perfect images by whatever means possible. This is what leads to the ethical conflict which engages the audience and makes the documentary interesting. Perhaps 'perfect' images can never be 'real'. It is a concept familiar to us today in the 21st century when many images in the media are manipulated and photoshopped.

Finally we need to consider the documentary as a whole and how effective these documentary techniques and ideas are over time. As a documentary it was timely as Hurley had regained popularity and his work was being reviewed and re-investigated as to its merit and relevance. How long do you think its shelf life or longevity is? How relevant will the documentary be in five years when the final group of students will be studying it for the HSC? Will the discoveries that the audience make from this documentary vary in their impact over time?

Perhaps we can leave the final word to the Australian government website and its summation of Hurley and his work. The words relate back to the issue of a text and its purpose.

> *'Hurley was a self-confessed showman'. He embellished images to maximise their visual impact, for example by using the technique of composite printing (combining the best elements of several shots into one). While such manipulation was common in pictorial photography, Hurley was criticised for using it to enhance documentary images.'*

HTTP://WWW.AUSTRALIA.GOV.AU/ABOUT-AUSTRALIA/AUSTRALIAN-STORY/FRANK-HURLEY

http://commons.wikimedia.org/wiki/File%3AWreck_of_the_'Gratitude'%2C_Macquarie_Island%2C_1911.jpg. By State Library of New South Wales collection from Australia (Wreck of the 'Gratitude', Macquarie Island, 1911) [see page for license], via Wikimedia Commons

Questions on Documentary Techniques

- Do you think the documentary is still relevant to a modern audience? Support your ideas with evidence from the text.
- List three examples of how manipulation of images has caused controversy in Hurley's work. How does Nasht present these in the documentary?
- Analyse the role interviews play in *Frank Hurley – The Man Who Made History* .What relevance do they have to Discovery?
- Discuss why Nasht uses original, archival Hurley footage in *Frank Hurley – The Man Who Made History.*What relevance does this technique have to Discovery?
- Analyse how the narrative of the story Nasht wants to tell unfolds. Do you think there is any bias in the telling of Hurley's story?
- What did you discover from your viewing of the documentary? Discuss ONE aspect in detail and show how Nasht conveys that discovery in *Frank Hurley – The Man Who Made History.*

THE ESSAY

The essay has been the subject of numerous texts and you should have the basic form well in hand. As teachers, the point we would emphasise would be to link the paragraphs both to each other and back to your argument (which should directly respond to the question). Of course, ensure your argument is logical and sustained.

Make sure you use specific examples and that your quotes are accurate. To ensure that you respond to the question make sure you plan carefully and are sure what relevant point each paragraph is making. Topic sentences are helpful to begin each paragraph and it is solid technique to actually 'tie up' each paragraph by linking it to the question.

When composing an essay the basic conventions of the form are:

- Address the question, state your argument, outline the points to be addressed and perhaps have a brief definition.

↓

A solid structure for each paragraph is:

- Topic sentence (*the main idea and its link to the previous paragraph/ argument*)
- Explanation/ discussion of the point including links between texts if applicable.
- Detailed evidence (*Close textual reference- quotes, incidents and technique discussion.*)
- Tie up by restating the point's relevance to argument/ question

↓

- Summary of points
- Final sentence that restates your argument

As well as this basic structure you will need to focus on:

Audience – for the essay the audience must be considered formal unless specifically stated otherwise. Therefore, your language must reflect the audience. This gives you the opportunity to use the jargon and vocabulary that you have learnt in English. For the audience ensure your introduction is clear and has impact. Avoid slang or colloquial language including contractions (doesn't, eg, etc).

Purpose – the purpose of the essay is to answer the question given. The examiner evaluates how well you can make an argument and understand the module's issues and its text(s). In the case of the Area of Study, markers look for a deep conceptual understanding and you must reveal understanding using examples from your prescribed text and a related text or texts. An essay is solidly structured so its composer can present ideas with clarity. This is where you earn marks. Essays do not retell the story of a text or state the obvious. They analyse rather than describe.

Communication – Take a few minutes to plan the essay. If you rush into your answer it is almost certain you will not make the most of the brief 40 minutes to show all you know about the question. More likely you will include irrelevant details that do not gain you marks but waste your precious time. Remember an essay is formal so do not do the following: story-tell, list and number points, misquote, use slang or colloquial language, be vague, use non sentences or fail to address the question.

HSC STYLE ESSAY QUESTION

Remember that essay responses must respond to essay questions and when you submit a practice essay, it should have a question written at the top. Start by underlining the key words in the question.

The Concept of Discovery may be conveyed differently in and through texts, but the result for responders is a deeper understanding of self and the world.

Discuss this statement with close reference to your prescribed text and two related texts.

PLAN

Introduction

Start by introducing the texts. ***Argument:*** The BOSTES definition for Discuss is to -Identify issues and provide points for and/or against. Consider using differing textual forms which affect how the concept of Discovery is conveyed. For example, a film will convey the concept of Discovery using visual, filmic techniques whereas a novel will use narrative techniques. Using a variety of textual forms will enable you to argue for the first half of the statement and enable you to show the different ways discovery is conveyed.

Having said this, you could argue that although specific techniques differ, the basic textual components of techniques, form, content and structure remain constant. Also consider the rubric and reflect on the different ways Discovery can be and are presented in your texts.

You need to let the marker know what texts you are discussing. You can start with a definition but it can come in the first paragraph of the body. You MUST state your argument in response to the question and the points you will cover as part of it. Don't wait until the end of the response to give it!

Do not forget the second part of the question, that is, the link to you as a responder and your deeper understanding of self and the world, through studying Discovery. You may like to argue that although text types and techniques differ and aspects of Discovery raised in and through texts differ, it is this variety which helps you as a responder relate the concept to your own understanding of the world and your place in it.

- (Aim to incorporate discussion of techniques when discussing text and making close textual references.)

↓

Idea 1– Look to the rubric and identify what kinds of Discovery are raised in your texts.

Idea 2- Explore how these are raised, through selected form and relevant techniques.

Idea 3 - Analyse their impact in terms of discovery on you as a responder. Is it a bildungsroman text. Do characters make personal discoveries, grow and learn? Is the composer him or herself a factor linked to a responder and discovery? Look at the purpose in writing the text. Explore these ideas in both your prescribed and related text or texts. In what ways have the aspects of Discovery raised in the three text enhanced your understanding of yourself and the world?

Ideas can be expanded into several paragraphs. be sure to set out paragraphs clearly using a topic sentence, explanation, examples and analysis of examples in terms of technique and link to question.

↓

Finally, your conclusion should incorporate a summary of key ideas. Do not raise new points in a conclusion.

- Provide a final sentence that restates your argument

Make sure your conclusion restates your argument. It does not have to be too long.

DISCOVERY: SUGGESTED RELATED TEXTS

You are often advised to select related texts that do not mirror the form of your Prescribed text. In addition, you are reminded to select related material wisely and look for links to the rubric, the concept and to highlight similarities and differences with prescribed material. Markers have noted that the judicious selection of related material is a key factor when evaluating responses. Sophisticated texts when well analysed in relation to the concept, and strongly analysed in relation to the prescribed text, will impress markers more than texts you may have happened to read at school in previous years in Stage Four or Five.

In the following list, categories are used for convenience but titles are not always exclusive to genre or text type. Many hybrid texts exist which cross boundaries of genre.

PROSE-FICTION/NON FICTION

Bypass – The Story of a Road by Michael McGirr

About one man's journey of discovery along the Hume Highway between Sydney and Melbourne. This is a hybrid text which is part travelogue, memoir, history and romance.

Gulliver's Travels by Jonathan Swift

This classic tale is about Gulliver's discovery of Lilliput. Through his arduous adventures he discovers lessons about society and humanity. The tale is a satirical view of the state of European government, and of petty differences between religions. It addresses the origins of human corruption, the conflict between Lilliputians and Yahoos, and other races.

A History of Reading by Alberto Manguel

Discover a personal response to books and reading and a love of literature. This is a wonderful non-fiction text written by an award winning author.

Looking for Alibrandi by Melina Marchetta

The aspect of discovery here is Alibrandi discovering who her estranged father is, as well as coping with various teenage issues in high school. This text is not as sophisticated as some other choices but it does raise aspects of culture and personal discovery.

Memoirs of a Geisha by Arthur Golden

This novel is about personal discovery and the development of identity in a tumultuous period in Japanese history.

My Place by Sally Morgan

This is a suitable text for Discovery. It is particularly focussed on personal/Cultural discovery.

The Secret River by Kate Grenville

Discover the interaction between the white settlers and the Aboriginal population on the Hawkesbury River. The discovery centres on place, people, including the composer, and cultures.

Small Island by Andrea Levy

Told by four narrators, the novel is set during the Second World War and tells the story of four different lives. There is racial tension and discovery of what it is like living with someone who comes from a different part of the world. Not only do you discover this new way of life, but it brings about a discovery of the self.

The Snowman by Jo Nesbo

Detective discovery in a European setting. This text presents modern take on the genre and is very well written.

So Much To Tell You by John Marsden

Here a scarred and introverted girl who is an elective mute, discovers a way to reveal her feelings to the reader in the form of a diary. In turn, readers discover Marina's life and relationships as she also discovers non-verbal ways to communicate with others.

Unpolished Gem by Alice Pung

In this text the Discovery theme involves cultural differences, migration and a new life for an Asian family in Footscray, Victoria. This text is about discovering life in a family and about cultures.

An Unsuitable Job for a Woman by P.D. James

Female detective Cordelia Gray investigates a suicide and a family with many secrets. The writing is detailed with plenty of atmosphere and clues. It is a crime fiction text, detection discovery with a twist. Consider other examples of Crime writing as discovery is a key theme within this genre.

FICTION / FILM

Alice in Wonderland (novel and film) original by Lewis Carroll

Alice discovers a magical fantasy world where she is in turmoil. Here she has amazing adventures and meets many intriguing characters.

Chronicles of Narnia (novel and film) original by C.S. Lewis

Four children, Peter, Suzan, Edmund and Lucy, discover a magical world behind their wardrobe and learn about their special role in saving the land from a great evil. The form of allegory can help responders discover deeper truths.

The Lost Thing (picture book and film) original by Shaun Tan

A boy discovers a lost thing and journeys to find it a home.

The Never-ending Story (novel and film) original by Michael Ende

The protagonist Sebastian discovers the world of Fantasia which is dying. He becomes part of the book he is reading and saves the world.

Sherlock Holmes (novel and film) original by Conan Doyle

Any of the *Sherlock Holmes* mysteries of adventures such as *The Hound of the Baskervilles* are recommended. These texts present discovery through means of deduction, calculation and scientific reasoning.

Under the Dome by Stephen King (novel and film)

Imagine being trapped and cut off from the world under a dome of power. This is a Science fiction text that is a long read but an intriguing idea. The initial discovery is awesome but then characters begin to discover things about themselves and others.

Where the Wild Things Are (picture book and film) original by Maurice Sendak

A young boy is punished by his mother and sent to his bedroom, which transforms into a jungle where he sails to an island and discovers that it is inhabited by malicious beasts known as the "Wild Things." After successfully intimidating the creatures, Max is hailed as the king of the Wild Things and enjoys a playful romp with his subjects. He discovers, however, that being king is not all fun. If you select a picture book, be sure to discuss visual literary techniques in a sophisticated manner.

Wizard of Oz (novel and film) original by Frank L. Baum

Dorothy discovers a magical fantasy world where various characters discover their true character. For example, Tin Man finds his heart.

The Book Thief by Marcus Zusak

A young orphaned girl meets her new family in Germany during the Second World War. Through the text the reader pieces together the story and discovers what is going on in the world around her. Historical discovery.

FILM

The Island directed by Michael Bay

Science fiction film about clones that live in a false utopian prison and discover their true origins as spare organ parts for wealthy but terminally ill people. The revelation is the discovery and how the discoverers respond to it.

It's Kind of a Funny Story directed by Ryan Fleck

A teenage boy checks himself into the mental ward only to find he has been relocated to the adult's ward. The film follows the boy and the friends he makes along the way.

50/50 directed by Jonathan Levine

Adam learns how to cope and live his life by coming to terms with his cancer.

An Education directed by Lone Sherfig

Jenny is in her final year of high school and has high hopes for the future when she meets a middle aged man who shows her another world. Jenny has to decide which world she wants to live in.

Consider also documentaries and other non fiction filmic forms.

POETRY

A suite of poems by a poet rather than one single poem is recommended, especially if the poem is brief.

'Easy Does It' by Bruce Dawe

A poem about discovering his boy and how he has to be 'careful' with him.

'Discovery' by Wislawa Szymborksa

The poem begins with 'I believe in the great discovery' and it is about faith and evidence.

'La Belle Dame Sans Merci' by John Keats

A knight discovers a new love and a new faery world but it is not what it seems and his discovery in this poem leads him to a life of misery.

'My Last Duchess' by Robert Browning

A dramatic monologue which reveals chilling and disturbing details about the speaker.

'Spring and Fall – To a Young Child' by Gerard Manley Hopkins

This is an address to a young girl, Margaret, and raises the discoveries that the child will make about the human condition. There is a prediction that these discoveries concerning life and death will be inevitable and with come with age and maturity.

SONGS

Remember that, if you write about a song, you are advised to consider more than just the lyrics.

At Seventeen by Janis Ian

Teen coming of age song about the angst of discovering what and who you are.

Kings and Queens by 30 Seconds to Mars

Discovering empowerment and greatness from despair.

Meant to Live by Switchfoot

Making the most out of life and discovering your absolute potential.

We Won't get Fooled Again by The Who

The persona in the song discovers that the new government which is established after a revolution is the same as the old government, and criticises it.

WEBSITES

100 Questions to Inspire Self-Discovery

HTTP://WWW.ALEXANDRAFRANZEN.COM/2013/04/18/100-QUESTIONS-TO-INSPIRE-RAPID-SELF-DISCOVERY/

Quite a few sites like this one that offer ideas on the topic. Read judiciously.

Discover the Extreme World

HTTP://WWW.MILESKELLY.NET/PRODUCTS-PAGE/DISCOVERY-EXPLORE-YOUR-WORLD/

Read the book blurb: Produced in association with Discovery Channel, this jam-packed book focuses on the extremes of core reference subjects. From animal giants to futuristic spy technology to the deepest caves and coldest places in the Universe. Nice change as it is aimed at children.

Discover Magazine

HTTP://AU.ZINIO.COM/MAGAZINE/DISCOVER/PR-500621662

Science based but has a wide range of articles on all sorts of interesting topics such as foods and environment.

HTTP://WWW.MILESKELLY.NET/PRODUCTS-PAGE/DISCOVERY-EXPLORE-YOUR-WORLD/

Discovery channel

HTTP://WWW.DISCOVERYCHANNEL.COM.AU/

Here you will discover many shows about discovery but it is also about learning.

Discovery Education

HTTP://WWW.DISCOVERYEDUCATION.COM/TEACHERS/

This address will lead you to the teacher resources but the site is full of content that shows another aspect of discovery i.e. education.

Famous People who Made Scientific Discoveries

HTTP://WWW.BIOGRAPHY.COM/PEOPLE/GROUPS/DISCOVERY/SCIENTIFIC

Another excellent source for evidence in film and written form on a comprehensive site.

Kids Discover

iPad app. Below is the address for the preview but you can download the app and use it. Excellent resource.

HTTPS://ITUNES.APPLE.COM/AU/APP/KIDS-DISCOVER/ID574832964?MT=8

The Science Channel

SCIENCE.DISCOVERY.COM/FAMOUS-SCIENTISTS-DISCOVERIES/100-GREATEST-DISCOVERIES.HTM

Almost complete collection of all the scientific discoveries covering most of the ancient and modern worlds in film and clearly explained.

Self Discovery

HTTP://EN.WIKIPEDIA.ORG/WIKI/JOURNEY_OF_SELF-DISCOVERY

Here are some definitions and links to the topic. A useful starting point to develop your ideas.